Track Changes

Easy Word Essentials
Volume 5

M.L. HUMPHREY

TITLES BY M.L. HUMPHREY

EASY WORD ESSENTIALS
Text Formatting
Page Formatting
Lists
Tables
Track Changes

WORD ESSENTIALS
Word for Beginners
Intermediate Word

MAIL MERGE ESSENTIALS
Mail Merge for Beginners

.

CONTENTS

INTRODUCTION

In *Word for Beginners* I covered the basics of working in Word and in *Intermediate Word* I covered more intermediate-level topics. But I realized that some users will just want to know about a specific topic and not buy a guide that covers a variety of other topics that aren't of interest to them.

So this series of guides is meant to address that need. Each guide in the series covers one specific topic such as formatting, tables, or track changes.

I'm going to assume in these guides that you have a basic understanding of how to navigate Word, although each guide does include an Appendix with a brief discussion of basic terminology to make sure that we're on the same page.

The guides are written using Word 2013, which should be similar enough for most users of Word to follow, but anyone using a version of Word prior to Word 2007 probably won't be able to use them effectively.

Also, keep in mind that the content in these guides is drawn from *Word for Beginners* and *Intermediate Word*, so if you think you'll end up buying all of these guides you're probably better off just buying *Word for Beginners* and *Intermediate Word* instead.

Having said all of that, let's talk track changes basics.

TRACK CHANGES

I love track changes. It is a fantastic tool and I'm not sure how I lived without it before it existed. You can write a document, give it to a group for review, they can make their changes in track changes, and you can easily see what they did. It's wonderful.

But...

Track Changes is also somewhat finicky. And it's changed with different versions of Word. I know that copy and paste have pretty much stayed the same for the last twenty years, for example. But that's not true of track changes.

This is probably one of the tools in Word that they like to mess with the most between releases. So the version of track changes you have in your version of Word probably isn't the same as the version I have. Especially if you have Word 2016.

It's a vital tool so we have to cover it. Just go into this knowing that some of how this works (how changes are shown, for example) will be the same, but other parts of it (your default document view or how multiple reviewers are handled) won't be.

OVERVIEW

Let's start with the basics. What is track changes? It's a way for you to see what changes have been made in a document and by whom they were made and when they were made. (So no telling your boss you were working late editing that document when you weren't. One little look at track changes will show you were actually done by four.)

Track changes is a great way to make changes and see changes that were made to plain text in your document. It can be a disaster (at least in older versions) to use track changes when editing tables or numbered lists or when working on formatting.

In my opinion.

(There will be some who strongly disagree with me, but I can't count the number of times I had to turn off track changes to wrestle a numbered list into shape or to really get a table looking the way it needed to. Not to mention, in some versions of Word changes to tables don't show as changes. You can delete a row or column and not have it shown as a change at all.)

So if you ever use track changes on a document, I highly recommend that you accept all changes in the document, turn off track changes entirely, and then do one final editing pass through the document. When I do this I inevitably find a few minor issues with formatting that need to be fixed and weren't readily visible in the track changes version—like a double period at the end of a sentence or an extra space after a numbered list. (The newer your version of Word, the less likely you'll need to do this, but it's a good habit to develop. Also, it makes sure you've turned off track changes, which is something you really really want to do for all documents.)

HOW TO

To turn Track Changes on, open your document and go to the Review tab. Choose Track Changes from the Track Changes dropdown in the Tracking section.

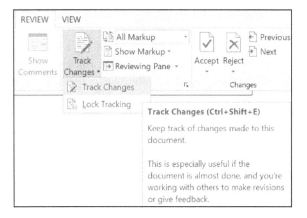

While track changes is turned on, any changes you make to the document will be tracked as a change to the document. Text that's been deleted will be shown as crossed out and be colored a different color based on the user who made the edit. Text that's been added will also be shown in a different color and underlined. For example:

> **This** is a test paragraph to sow you how track changes works. See how I misspelled show there?
>
> **This** is a test paragraph to show you how track changes works. See how I misspelled show there?
>
> When you make edits or add new text with track changes on, it looks something like this and a line appears on the left where changes were made.

Here I started with the first line of text and copied it. I then turned on track changes and added an h to the word show. It was marked in red and underlined. (Only for track changes. If I were to accept the change, that h I added would be in black text and without an underline, just like the text that surrounds it. This is one of the reasons I recommend accepting all changes and reading through your document one last time. I've seen text that was added to a document that was underlined by the user, but no one could tell that until all changes were accepted.)

You can also see in the example above where I deleted a question from what I had copied. That text is marked in red and crossed out.

The new text I added in the last paragraph is also marked in red.

Now, something to be aware of. I have worked with people who saw track changes, didn't understand how it works in Word, and so manually created their own version of track changes by formatting their edits to look like track changes. Rather than use track changes they would manually format the text they wanted to delete with a strikethrough, for example. That meant the text wasn't actually deleted. It was just reformatted.

NEVER, EVER DO THAT. Now that you've read this guide I expect you to understand that that is an awful way to show changes in your document. If you ever do that someone will have to manually go through the document and remove or reformat every single edit and they will hate you for it. Not to mention how much extra time and effort is required to do that. Just turn on track changes when you start to review the document and all of your edits will be recorded. If you mess it up and don't use track changes, then use document compare to have Word flag all of your edits for you. But never, never, never manually format your text to show the edits you want. That's something that was maybe necessary thirty years ago, but certainly is not now.

Also, if you're working with someone who isn't very familiar with Word, keep an eye out for this. I'm hoping we're past when people would do that, but we probably aren't. And the people most likely to do it are the most senior-level folks who you can't exactly make fix it themselves.

TRACK CHANGES VIEWS

It's the default in Word 2013 to show the final version of your document without the track changes visible and with only a small mark off to the side to indicate that a change has been made in the document. Personally, I hate that. I suppose it's good in theory because you get to see what the final product looks like without having to parse through what's been changed. And you're less likely to miss things like a double period that can be hard to catch when tracked changes are visible in the document.

But not being able to see the changes in a document can make reviewing edits tricky. At work I need to see each and every change made in a document to confirm that I agree, even the most minor one. In my day job area of expertise (financial regulation), it matters what words are used. Not to mention, comma placement can be crucial.

Because of this I always change my view so I can see the original version of the document with all changes visible.

(I also think it's important to remember that track changes are in place in a document. As you'll see in a second, there's a track changes view that doesn't show any indication that track changes are on. Problem with that view is if someone doesn't realize track changes are on and sends a document on to a client with those changes still in there and the client is able to see all of the changes. It can get ugly when that happens.)

Anyway.

There are four choices of view available in track changes. To access them, go to the Tracking section of the Review tab. You should see a dropdown menu on the top right of that section. Depending on your current view it will either say Simple Markup, No Markup, All Markup, or Original.

Here is an example of the text from above in each view.

Original

This is a test paragraph to sow you how track changes works. See how I misspelled show there?

This is a test paragraph to sow you how track changes works. See how I misspelled show there?

Simple Markup

This is a test paragraph to sow you how track changes works. See how I misspelled show there?

This is a test paragraph to show you how track changes works.

When you make edits or add new text with track changes on, it looks something like this and a line appears on the left where changes were made.

All Markup

This is a test paragraph to sow you how track changes works. See how I misspelled show there?

This is a test paragraph to s̲how you how track changes works. ~~See how I misspelled show there?~~

<u>When you make edits or add new text with track changes on, it looks something like this and a line appears on the left where changes were made.</u>

No Markup

This is a test paragraph to sow you how track changes works. See how I misspelled show there?

This is a test paragraph to show you how track changes works.

When you make edits or add new text with track changes on, it looks something like this and a line appears on the left where changes were made.

It may be a little hard to see, so let me also describe each view for you. Original shows what the text looked like before I turned on Track Changes. None of the changes that have been made in the document are visible. This can be a useful view if you want to see what a document looked like before people started mucking around with it, but that's really the only time you should use it.

Simple Markup has a red line off to the left side of the text. This line indicates that changes were made to the text on that line, but you can't tell what changes were made. The text you see on the page is the final text after all edits.

All Markup (my preferred view) has a line off to the left side of the text to indicate that changes have been made, but also shows those changes in the text of the document. So you can see that I've added text and deleted text and what text I've added and deleted.

No Markup is the most dangerous view in my opinion. It shows the final text with no indication that track changes is on or that changes have been made at that point in the document. It can have its uses. You can use it to see what the final document will look like with all changes incorporated. But I would highly, highly recommend that you never leave your document in this view. Use it and immediately change it back. And if you work with someone who uses this setting, be sure to always check any document before you send it on as a final document to make sure that track changes have been turned off and all changes in the document have been accepted.

SHOW MARKUP DROPDOWN

I should note that none of the views showed the formatting change I made to the word "This" in the first line. I bolded that text and yet none of them indicate that I did that. (In older versions of Word the change probably would be visible, but not in Word 2013.)

To see formatting changes in your document, go to the Tracking section of the Review pane and click on Show Markup to bring up the dropdown menu. From there go to Balloons which will bring up a secondary dropdown menu. Select the Show Only Comments And Formatting In Balloons option. This will add indications off to the side when formatting changes have been made in the document.

The default show markup view is Show All Revisions Inline which clearly doesn't work if you want to see formatting revisions. It also doesn't show comments (which we'll cover in a minute) in their entirety. They're just indicated by a small set of initials in brackets within the document. I would recommend always having your comments visible to the side since that's where a lot of the explanations and back and forth between reviewers occurs. (Or at least where it should.)

(Another show markup option is to Show Revisions in Balloons, which in my sample here looks exactly like Show Only Comments and Formatting In Balloons.)

If I change my view to show comments and formatting in balloons, it looks like this:

Now you can finally see all of the edits that have been made to the document with the indicator on the right-hand side showing that I bolded the word "This" in the document.

The way I would recommend you review any document is with All Markup selected and Comments and Formatting In Balloons selected. (And if you find you don't want to see formatting edits at all, you can turn that off in the Show Markup dropdown menu by clicking on formatting to uncheck it.) Only use the other options for very specific purposes and then always change it back.

CHANGES BY MULTIPLE USERS

Unless something is off about the settings on your document, each individual user who makes changes to the document will be assigned a different color for their changes. When it's just one person making edits to the document using track changes, those changes are generally shown in red. The next user is in blue, etc., etc. This isn't based on who the user is, so you can be assigned the color red in one document and green in another. If you hold your mouse over any specific change, Word will tell you who the user was who made the changes and when they made them.

(If your document has been stripped of personalization, it's possible to have all changes in the document show up under Author and to not be able to tell who made what change. I would highly recommend that you do not strip personalization from a document that you intend to continue working on. Or that if you have to do so that you also save a version that hasn't had personalization stripped.

It's horrible to work on a group document when all changes are marked as by Author.)

Also, if for some reason someone hasn't customized their version of Word (which is rare in corporate settings and probably impossible in newer versions of Word) the changes they make will show up as Author. If you happen to have two users who have done this, their changes will be combined under the same color and user name.

REVIEWING PANES

Track changes also gives you the option of using something called reviewing panes. Review panes list all formatting changes, insertions, deletions, and comments. You can have one visible either below the document (horizontal) or off to the side of the document (vertical).

Usually reviewing panes aren't visible unless you choose to open them, but sometimes they will appear automatically. (I want to say this happens when there are so many comments in a section that they aren't easy to see otherwise.)

If you want to see a reviewing pane, go to the Tracking section of the Review tab and choose the type of reviewing pane you want from the Reviewing Pane dropdown menu. This will insert a new window on your screen that lists all of the changes that have been made to the document.

The reviewing panes can be useful, but I almost never use them. For example, when I bolded "This" the reviewing pane indicates that something was bolded at that point in the document, but it doesn't say what. Whereas when I turn on the option to see formatting changes in a balloon there's a dotted line pointing to the text that was changed.

SEEING PREVIOUS AND NEXT CHANGES

Now that we have the settings the way we want them (for me that's all markup and comments and formatting in balloons), it's time to review the changes that were made in the document.

If I'm just reviewing changes to a document, I will walk through the document by using the Previous and Next options in the Changes section of the Review tab.

To do this, start at the beginning of your document and click Next. That will take you to the next change that was made in the document and will highlight it for you so you can review it. This approach lets you catch even the smallest edits. If you just scan your document for different colored text, you're very likely to miss changes to punctuation. (You can scan for the mark on the left-hand side of the page that indicates a change was made instead, but even that isn't perfect. If there was a larger edit and a smaller edit in the same paragraph you may only see the larger edit.)

And be sure to go through the entire document. If you don't start on the first page, you need to make sure you continue through to where you did start your review.

ACCEPT OR REJECT CHANGES

Using Previous and Next will show you the changes that were made in your document but will also leave them in the document still marked as changes.

The other option for walking through a document is to use the Accept or Reject options in the Changes section of the Review tab. This will accept or reject the changes as you review them and remove them from being visible changes to the document.

I generally don't use them this way. What I do is review all changes in a document and if I'm happy with all of them, and it's my role to do so, I accept all changes at the end of my review. If I run into a change I don't like, I'll make further edits to the document to make it acceptable or I'll reject it at that point.

But if you do want to accept changes as you move through the document, go to the Changes section of the Review tab, and click on the dropdown next to Accept. You'll see that you have a number of available options:

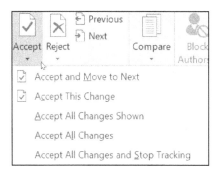

(The options for Reject are the same except using Reject in place of Accept.)

The option I would use if I was walking through a document and accepting changes as I went is Accept And Move To Next. This accepts the change you're currently on and moves to the next change in the document. If you reach a change that you don't want to keep, then you would choose Reject And Move To Next from the Reject dropdown.

If you're going to do it this way, be careful with sections that have multiple changes. Sometimes you'll accept a change but it won't accept all changes that were made to that section and you'll need to do it a few times to accept all of the changes. (Same goes for rejecting changes.)

Basically, if you're accepting or rejecting changes and you're not doing it for all changes at once, be sure that the text appears the way you want it to before you move on.

(I should note, too, that when using Previous and Next I have on occasion accepted all changes on a section to make sure that it will appear the way I expect and then used Ctrl + Z to undo that so I could just accept all changes once at the very end. You could probably use the No Markup view and get the same outcome.)

And one more note: Be careful when rejecting edits. If you review a document and reject an edit, Word doesn't show that an edit was made and then later rejected. So no one is going to know about that edit. It's just gone. When working on large group projects this can be a problem. I once saw someone very senior make an edit that was rejected by a junior staff member who thought they knew what they were doing and didn't. Because the edit and subsequent rejection of the edit didn't show in the document, no one on the team knew about it. Fortunately, someone else on the team caught the issue in a read-through, but that may not always happen. If I think it's important that someone see and approve it, I will edit an edit instead of reject it. (Or you can add a comment to the document indicating that you just rejected the edit.)

TURNING OFF TRACK CHANGES

Always turn off track changes when you're done with editing a document. There's nothing worse than making a few last-minute changes and having them show up in track changes and not catching it.

To turn off track changes, go to the Tracking section of the Review tab and click on Track Changes to bring up the dropdown menu and then click on Track Changes. (You can also use Ctrl + Shift + E to turn track changes on and off.)

If you still have changes tracked in your document, turning off track changes will leave those changes the way they are (marked as changes), but any edits you make to the document from that point forward will not show as changes. Be very careful about doing that, though. It's easy to turn off track changes and forget that you did it and then send on a document to someone else for review and have them not see all of the changes you made.

I do turn off track changes when I'm working on edits to complex multi-level lists and sometimes with tables, too, because it's just easier to work without track changes on, but when I do this I will usually run a document compare at the very end and provide that to anyone who needs to review my edits so that they can see all changes that were made.

TRACK CHANGES WITH TABLES, LISTS, AND FORMATTING

As I just mentioned, I tend to turn off track changes when I need to do a lot of formatting changes or when I'm working with tables or multi-level lists. One reason is because when you make a lot of formatting changes they can get overwhelming and generally don't matter to anyone else. No one needs to see that the spacing of that paragraph was changed, they just need to know it now matches the rest of the paragraphs. (And the folks that don't want to see all of that are usually also the ones that don't know how to turn it off themselves.)

The other main reason is because Word wasn't always as good at tracking changes as it is now. In older versions of Word I simply couldn't get tables or numbered lists to look like what I wanted if I was editing them in track changes. The minute I accepted all changes something would be off. (And I can't say with 100% certainty that there still aren't issues with newer versions of Word. So to save myself the headache, I turn it off, do what I need to do, and then do a document compare for anyone who needs to see what I've done.)

CONCLUSION

So that's the basics of track changes in Word.
   If you get stuck, reach out at:

mlhumphreywriter@gmail.com

I'm happy to help. I don't check that email account every single day but I do check it regularly and will try to find you the answer if I don't know it.
   Good luck with it!

APPENDIX A: BASIC TERMINOLOGY

TAB

I refer to the menu choices at the top of the screen (File, Home, Insert, Design, Page Layout, References, Mailings, Review, View, Developer) as tabs. If you click on one you'll see that the way it's highlighted sort of looks like an old-time filing system.

CLICK

If I tell you to click on something, that means to use your mouse (or trackpad) to move the arrow on the screen over to a specific location and left-click or right-click on the option. (See the next definition for the difference between left-click and right-click).

If you left-click, this selects the item. If you right-click, this generally creates a dropdown list of options to choose from. If I don't tell you which to do, left- or right-click, then left-click.

LEFT-CLICK/RIGHT-CLICK

If you look at your mouse or your trackpad, you generally have two flat buttons to press. One is on the left side, one is on the right. If I say left-click that means to press down on the button on the left. If I say right-click that means press down on the button on the right.

Now, as I sadly learned when I had to upgrade computers and ended up with an HP Envy, not all track pads have the left- and right-hand buttons. In that case, you'll basically want to press on either the bottom left-hand side of the track pad or the bottom right-hand side of the trackpad. Since you're working blind it may take a little trial and error to get the option you want working. (Or is that just me?)

SELECT OR HIGHLIGHT

If I tell you to select text, that means to left-click at the end of the text you want to select, hold that left-click, and move your cursor to the other end of the text you want to select.

Another option is to use the Shift key. Go to one end of the text you want to select. Hold down the shift key and use the arrow keys to move to the other end of the text you want to select. If you arrow up or down, that will select an entire row at a time.

With both methods, which side of the text you start on doesn't matter. You can start at the end and go to the beginning or start at the beginning and go to the end. Just start at one end or the other of the text you want to select.

The text you've selected will then be highlighted in gray.

If you need to select text that isn't touching you can do this by selecting your first section of text and then holding down the Ctrl key and selecting your second section of text using your mouse. (You can't arrow to the second section of text or you'll lose your already selected text.)

DROPDOWN MENU

If you right-click in a Word document, you will see what I'm going to refer to as a dropdown menu. (Sometimes it will actually drop upward if you're towards the bottom of the document.)

A dropdown menu provides you a list of choices to select from.

There are also dropdown menus available for some of the options listed under the tabs at the top of the screen. For example, if you go to the Home tab, you'll see small arrows below or next to some of the options, like the numbered list option in the paragraph section. If you click on those arrows, you'll see that there are multiple choices you can choose from listed on a dropdown menu.

DIALOGUE BOX

Dialogue boxes are pop-up boxes that cover specialized settings. As just mentioned, if you click on an expansion arrow, it will often open a dialogue box that contains more choices than are visible in that section. When you right-click in a Word document and choose Font, Paragraph, or Hyperlink that also opens dialogue boxes.

Dialogue boxes allow the most granular level of control over an option. For example, the Paragraph Dialogue Box has more options available than in the Paragraph section of the Home tab.

(This may not apply to you, but be aware that if you have more than one Word document open and open a dialogue box in one of those documents, you may not be able to move to the other documents you have open until you close the dialogue box.)

CONTROL SHORTCUTS

I'll occasionally mention control shortcuts that you can use to perform tasks. When I reference them I'll do so by writing it as Ctrl + a capital letter. To use the shortcut just hold down the control key while typing the letter specified. Even though the letter will be capitalized, you don't need to use the capitalized version for the shortcut to work. For example, holding down the Ctrl key and the s key at the same time will save your document. I'll write this as Ctrl + S.

ABOUT THE AUTHOR

M.L. Humphrey is a former stockbroker with a degree in Economics from Stanford and an MBA from Wharton who has spent close to twenty years as a regulator and consultant in the financial services industry.

You can reach M.L. at mlhumphreywriter@gmail.com or at mlhumphrey.com.

Track changes is a great tool for working collaboratively in Word and almost essential for identifying and discussing changes to a document in a group setting. But in order to use it effectively, you have to understand it.

That's what this guide will do for you.

ISBN 978-1-950902-29-3
50799